o Throw a

Great Derby Party

Sue Wylie

ILLUSTRATIONS BY Chris Ware

Lexington, Kentucky

ECLIPSE
PRESS

Copyright © 2008 Blood-Horse Publications

All rights reserved. No part of this book may be reproduced in
any form by any means, including photocopying, audio recording,
or any information storage or retrieval system, without the
permission in writing from the copyright holder.
Inquiries should be addressed to Publisher, Blood-Horse Publications,
Box 919003, Lexington, KY 40591-9003.

Library of Congress Control Number: 2007941682

ISBN 978-1-58150-180-3

Printed in China
First Edition: 2008

a division of
Blood-Horse Publications
PUBLISHERS SINCE 1916

Contents

Introduction

UNIVERSAL APPEAL

Kentuckians are used to it. It happens to them all the time. Whenever and wherever they travel outside their Bluegrass state, just as soon as they say where they are from, strangers' faces will break into smiles and heads will nod in approval.

"Oh, yes! The Kentucky Derby," they exclaim, their voices rich with respect.

It happens to Kentuckians in places all over the world: in a café in Paris or at a restaurant in Rome, on a Caribbean cruise or aboard a plane high above the Andes. Everyone, it seems, knows about the Kentucky Derby, which clearly lives up to its billing as "the most famous horse race in the world."

The Derby may belong to Kentucky, but its fame and fans are universal. It thrills and fascinates people who don't know a horse's

The Kentucky Derby ... "the most famous horse race in the world."

hoof from a horse's haunch or who have never set foot on a race-track, people whose only experience with equines has been a ride on a merry-go-round. On those popular lists of "things I want to do before I die," it's not unusual for people to put "go to the Kentucky Derby" near the top. Even the Queen of England said it was her life-long dream. The monarch finally got her wish in 2007 when she and Prince Philip were the guests of honor at Churchill Downs for the Run for the Roses.

But, alas, for the rest of us, actually attending the Derby can be difficult. Tickets are very expensive and very scarce. Churchill Downs can pack in more than 150,000 fans, but that leaves everyone else to find other ways to celebrate Kentucky's most cherished tradition. So, on the first Saturday in May, all across the nation, millions of people

Derby Day positively zings with excitement and sparkles with hospitality.

crowd around television screens to watch breathlessly "the greatest two minutes in sports." They clap wildly, cheer loudly, and get a trifle misty-eyed when the Churchill Downs crowd sings "My Old Kentucky Home." In 2007 more than fifty-four million people in the United States tuned in to see Street Sense dash to victory.

Watching the race with friends and with a mint julep in hand is even more fun, so each year more and more fans decide to pay tribute to the event by hosting a Derby party. So many, in fact, that next to Super Bowl Sunday and New Year's Eve, Kentucky Derby Day has become the nation's most popular home-party day of the year. Such soirées sprinkle the nation from coast to coast. Many are hosted by nostalgic transplanted Kentuckians; others, by folks who have no Kentucky connections but are intrigued by the Derby's deep, beautiful traditions.

"Please, please, do this again next year!"

The first Saturday in May is not an official state holiday in Kentucky, but it certainly feels like one. Derby Day positively zings with excitement and sparkles with hospitality. It's a day completely unique, crowded with festivities, fanfare, and fun; a day to dress up and do something special; a day to go to a party where men sport ice cream-colored silk blazers and women wear wispy spring dresses and fabulous hats.

The parties are "off and running" early in the morning with thousands of Kentuckians turning out for the Governor's Derby Breakfast, to which the public is invited for ham, eggs, grits, and a glimpse of the governor himself. For the rest of the day, brunches, lunches, picnics, barbecues, cocktail parties, dinners, and dances abound. (It takes stamina, but some sturdy folks actually manage to cram all of these events into their social calendar.) Kentuckians have been throwing Derby parties since 1875, when the race was born, and practice does make perfect, as they say. No wonder, then, that Derby party hosts everywhere look to Kentucky for ideas and inspiration.

This book is your invitation to a Kentucky Derby party — your own! Yes, you are about to take the Derby party plunge and join the growing ranks of gracious hosts who celebrate the most famous horse race in the world. You've already got the date — the first Saturday in May. Now all you need to do is to make sure your guests have such a good time that they will beg you to "Please, please, do this again next year!" You want your Derby party to be a winner in every way, and this little book will help you make that happen. It's full of ideas and tips on how to feed, entertain, surprise, and delight your guests from party starting gate to finish line!

Chapter One

A GRAND TRADITION

The Kentucky Derby is one of America's greatest annual events, as American as "Yankee Doodle Dandy," and as a Derby party host, you will be carrying on a grand old tradition.

No one seems to know for certain when the very first Derby party was held, but the Derby itself was initially run on May 17, 1875, before a crowd of 10,000 in Louisville at the Jockey Club track, which would later become Churchill Downs. The track was the brainchild of Colonel Meriwether Lewis Clark Jr., grandson of William Clark of the Lewis and Clark expedition. A racing enthusiast, he organized the Jockey Club, whose mission was to raise the money to build the racetrack.

There were some ecstatic press reviews for the inaugural race and the track facilities, but no one mentioned any pre- or post-race party. The writer for the *Kentucky Live Stock Record* verbally drooled in his account of the day.

"The morning broke without a visible cloud in the heavens, while a cool breeze was wafted over the course ... The portion of the grandstand devoted to the ladies was one grand bouquet of beauty, refinement, and intelligence. The ladies in their various colored costumes looked like so many parti-colored butterflies, balancing themselves on their wings, in the slanting rays of the bright sun."

Could it be that some of those ladies had brought along picnic baskets, filled with fried chicken or biscuits and country ham to constitute the first Derby party?

The originator could easily have been the legendary Colonel Matt J. Winn, who early on encouraged private Derby parties.

As home of the Kentucky Derby, Kentucky
is famed for its Derby parties. Well-known
socialites Marylou Whitney and Anita Madden
helped create the Derby party mystique.

He was a genius in making anything and everything about the Derby appeal to the public. Winn was the Louisville businessman, promoter, and marketing wizard who saved Churchill Downs from bankruptcy in 1902 by forming a new management team and giving up his very successful men's clothing store to become vice president and general manager of the track. He traveled the nation, ballyhooing the excitement and romance of the Derby and creating many of its traditions: the playing of "My Old Kentucky Home," the blanket of red roses for the winner, and the special Kentucky Derby glasses for mint juleps.

The Kentucky Derby is the first leg of Thoroughbred racing's Triple Crown, but in the social hierarchy it far and away outshines the Preakness and the Belmont. As home of the Derby, Kentucky is famed for its Derby parties, but it was mainly the imagination, hospitality, and glamour of two exceptionally wealthy, renowned women that made Derby Eve in Kentucky so uniquely dazzling that society reporters and TV crews from all over the world flocked into Lexington to cover the alluring hostesses and their rich and famous guests.

Socialites and horsewomen Marylou Whitney and Anita Madden, mistress of Hamburg Place (which has bred five Kentucky Derby winners), are longtime friends, but for more than thirty years, come Derby Eve, they would compete for the title of "Hostess with the Most-est." Both held lavish, glittering galas at their Lexington estates where long lines of limousines unloaded cargoes of Hollywood stars and international celebrities from the worlds of entertainment, politics, and sports.

At the Whitney Farm, stars such as Diane Sawyer, Walter Cronkite, Gregory Peck, Ivana Trump, and Joan Rivers sat their elegantly clad derrières down to dinner on gilt, velvet-padded chairs in the poolside atrium, washed down Kentucky fried chicken and corn pudding with French champagne, and danced the night away to the well-mannered music of Lester Lanin.

Across town, at the Madden farm, thousands (yes, thousands!) of townspeople and out-of-towners partied uninhibitedly under a huge red tent and boogied on the dance floor till dawn, hip-to-hip with big-name, show-biz personalities while top bands blared their rock music.

Both parties began as small, private pre-Derby get-togethers for a few houseguests, but each year they grew bigger and the invitations grew more coveted. Finally, the parties became victims of their own successes. When Madden's guest list for her sit-down dinner-dance hit 3,200 people, she decided it was time to call it a night. That was in 1998, but to this day Madden still receives letters and e-mails from disappointed former guests from around the world urging her to "bring back your fabulous party. There's never been anything like it."

*The Barnstable-Brown party
is now the most famous Derby Eve party,
attended by celebrities, royalty,
and wannabes.*

The Derby Eve hostess crown in Kentucky has now been passed on to the Barnstable twins, Priscilla and Patricia. Remember them? They were once the Doublemint Gum twins of TV commercial fame. Now they are the hosts of the "hottest" of Derby Eve parties. Thousands of guests turn out for the big bash on the sweeping grounds of the Louisville mansion where Patricia Barnstable Brown resides with her husband. This party, which is a charity event for diabetes research, is *the* place to be seen on Derby Eve. It is also the place to see. Hundreds of the uninvited gather outside the residence, hoping to catch a peek of arriving celebrities. The guest list is packed with names such as Rod Stewart, Pamela Anderson, Kid Rock, Travis Tritt, and Prince Albert of Monaco. Actually, this party could be famous for one reason alone: It's where the late Anna Nicole Smith met Larry Birkhead, the Louisville man whom the courts declared in a world-publicized case after Smith's death to be the father of her daughter.

Of course, super-sized, star-studded, spare-no-cost parties on the scale of those flamboyant three are as rare as rubies. Meanwhile, across Kentucky and the rest of the nation, legions of hosts are throwing much smaller, more modest, but simply terrific Derby parties. Many of these become annual traditions, eagerly looked forward to all year long by both hosts and guests.

Along about February each year, the phone begins to ring more often than usual at the Richmond, Kentucky, home of April and Clark Pergrem. The anxious callers just want to be reassured that the couple will be hosting their famous Kentucky Derby party again this year, won't they? To their relief, the Pergrems' answer, for a number of years now, has been "absolutely, yes!"

This party at the Pergrems is an event that gets rave reviews all year long. The guests are still talking, and very understandably, about the time one partygoer won — Wow! — *$15,000* in the clever "horse auctions" that Clark has set up. You could use his idea to add a lot of excitement to your own party (but first check your state's laws governing such games of chance).

Here's how it works. Just before the Derby is run, each horse is auctioned off to the highest bidder. Two separate auctions are held to give more people a chance to "own" a Derby contender. The bidder whose horse wins the Derby gets *all* of the money bid on *all* of the horses in his auction. Clark says one lucky guest's winnings over the past three parties is close to $30,000!

The party started out seven years ago with about fifty people invited to watch the Derby and enjoy a casual buffet. Now, two hundred guests spill out of the house and into the poolside pavilion and even into the guesthouse. There are TV sets going in almost every room of the main house, plus a 50-inch plasma on the patio. The Pergrems decided to keep this a casual Derby party in every way; no dressing up is required for the guests, and April's buffet menu is

> *There are TV sets going in almost every room of the main house, plus a 50-inch plasma on the patio.*

always familiar "comfort foods" such as fried chicken, fried fish, and hamburgers. Tables for ten hold centerpieces of red roses and baby's breath in julep cups.

Guests begin arriving at 3 p.m. and have such a good time that many stay till 11 p.m., so April keeps the bar and the buffet going all afternoon and evening.

There's a charming annual tradition at the party thanks to the Pergrems' daughter, Madison. For the very first party, when she was just 4 years old, she decorated a fancy Derby hat, all by herself, and then auctioned it off to the guests, all by herself. The winning bid was $100, which she donated to charity. Madison's Derby hat and her auctioneering have been a party feature ever since.

Maybe, just maybe, an Academy Award-winning set designer could come up with a more perfect setting for a Kentucky Derby party than the one used by Dr. Phillip Tibbs and his wife, Trudy, but that's doubtful. It would certainly be challenging, maybe even impossible, to dream up anything more beautifully appropriate than their Forest Retreat estate, a magnificent historic treasure with past ties to the horse industry.

The house, in Carlisle, Kentucky, was built in 1814 by Thomas Metcalfe, a former Kentucky governor. Over the years the estate fell into shabbiness until 1933, when it was rescued and lovingly restored by Dr. Eslie Asbury, a founding member of Keeneland Race Course in Lexington. In fact, he bred the 1954 Kentucky Derby winner, Determine.

In 2001 the Tibbses bought Forest Retreat and glowingly transformed it. Since 2004 it has been the site of their Derby Day party and *what* a party! The Tibbses say they consider it their "signature social event."

> *Women wear dresses, hats, and even white gloves, those archaic relics of ladylike fashion; men don white linen suits or blazers and bow ties.*

All 180 guests are garbed in "Derby attire" as specified on the invitation: Women wear dresses, hats, and even white gloves, those archaic relics of ladylike fashion; men don white linen suits or blazers and bow ties.

"We were thrilled," Dr. Tibbs said, "when a guest from North Carolina showed up in a snow-white silk suit, a bowler hat, and swinging a gold cane."

All afternoon the crowd is treated to nonstop Derby culture, starting with Trudy's "special mint juleps," made with her own mint syrup and garnished with fresh mint from her garden. CDs of Kentucky songs supply tunes such as "Run for the Roses" by Dan Fogelberg.

The betting is brisk but very basic. "We use the honor system," Dr. Tibbs explained. "There is an envelope for every one of the Derby horses. Guests watch the track odds on the TV sets, and to bet they simply put however much money they choose into the envelope and write their name and the amount of their bet on it. All of the money bet goes into one big pot and is split among everyone who bet on the winner. That's it. No place bets, no show bets. The winners take all."

At 5:30 p.m., the doctor plays a recording ("very loudly," he says) of the bugle call to the post and leads the guests into a big tent that measures 100 by 40 feet. They stand with their hands over their hearts and listen to a recording of former Kentucky Governor Happy Chandler's famous rendition of "My Old Kentucky Home."

Dinner is an elegant buffet of traditional Derby food. There's always an abundance of fried chicken, cheese grits, and Derby pie. Guests dine at twenty tables bearing lush centerpieces. For these, Trudy buys twenty-dozen American Beauty roses.

The party is so popular that some of the guests have done an almost unheard of thing and given away their so-coveted and so-expensive Derby tickets. "We'd rather be here," they say, and that is the supreme compliment for a Derby party host.

Chapter Three

FAR FROM MY OLD KENTUCKY HOME

Every spring, as sure as the return of the robins, hordes of transplanted Kentuckians come down with acute cases of Derby fever. The symptoms include deep sighs of nostalgia, recurring visions of the crowds at Churchill Downs, and a sudden thirst for a mint julep. The common cure for this annual affliction is a Derby party, and so, on the first Saturday in May, the nation is sprinkled coast to coast with such celebrations hosted by former Kentuckians. You may want to take some of their ideas for your own party.

It's only June and the next Kentucky Derby is still almost a full year away, but already Mac Riley is deep in phone calls, Post-it notes, and plans for his Kentucky Society of Washington's annual pre-Derby party. After all, when you're expecting 1,300 — maybe as many as 1,500 — guests and when you are a host for what's called the largest and most prestigious Derby party in the nation, you'd *better* have started planning a long time ago.

In private life Riley is an attorney/businessman in Virginia. In public life he is the president of the Kentucky Society of Washington, an organization made up of former Kentuckians now living in the D.C. area. That position makes him the unofficial host of the society's famous annual pre-Derby party.

For more than a quarter of a century, society members have been getting together on the Saturday before the Derby to kick off the formal week of festivities. The party began very modestly, decades ago, with about seventy-five

people meeting in someone's backyard to drink mint juleps and schmooze about what was going on back in Kentucky. Today, the mammoth party is held in Arlington, Virginia, on the sprawling grounds of the historic Collingswood Estate on the banks of the Potomac River. Invitations are limited due to space to Society members and their guests.

"If we had the room, we could sell six thousand tickets," Riley said. "*Everyone* wants to be there. This party is one of the highlights of the Washington social season. This is truly an extravaganza."

Indeed, each year Riley has to figure out the most diplomatic way of telling a government VIP, "Sorry, there are no tickets and no room" left for the Society's much-heralded party.

The guest list is stunningly high-powered, heavy with members of Congress, cabinet secretaries, business magnates, social giants, and television personalities. These dressed-up VIPs stroll along the

Potomac, wander through the mansion, drink juleps made with good Kentucky bourbon, and fill up on — what else — beef tenderloin, biscuits with country ham, and Benedictine sandwiches, the very same things you can serve your guests at your Derby party!

When Jeremy Lang was growing up in Kentucky's capital city, Frankfort, Derby parties were always part of his family's life. When he moved to San Francisco to study architecture, he couldn't wait to introduce his new West Coast friends to his beloved Derby culture.

"The Derby party is a unique, dramatic way to celebrate a great tradition and being from Kentucky," Lang said. "A Derby party is so unlike any other American event."

For Lang's first California party, his e-mail invitations specified a very strict dress code. The men *must* wear summer suits (seersucker, if possible) and neckties. The women *must* wear spring cocktail dresses and *hats*. Imagine that! But on Derby Day, one hundred very properly dressed guests showed up at Lang's apartment, and they have been coming back every Derby Day since.

His party is now an annual, anticipated event for his friends who take the dressing-up very seriously and vie to be selected as "best dressed" by the judges Lang picks from among his guests. The natty winners are presented with prizes of Kentucky bourbon and bourbon ball candy.

Almost all the party food comes from Kentucky, Lang said proudly. He orders the country ham online; the Kentucky beer cheese and smoked turkey come from the famous Pink Pig Barbecue restaurant in Frankfort; and the Derby Pie is the authentic kind from Kern's Kitchen in Louisville. Lang makes his own mint syrup for the juleps, which he serves in his collection of vintage Derby glasses.

"The juleps are always a big hit," he said. "The only thing that's ever bombed was the burgoo. Everyone thought it was beef stew."

The betting started out as "winner-take-all" pots, but guests soon clamored for more exotic options, so Lang now makes up poster-sized charts showing the Derby contenders, their jockeys, and earnings. He sets up an odds-based pool that's split among winning bettors.

Now a veteran host, Lang has every detail of his party down pat. He orders official Derby programs from Churchill Downs for his guests to take home as souvenirs, and he has printed up copies of the lyrics to "My Old Kentucky Home" to pass out. No excuses — everyone must join in the post-time rendition.

Now, Lang has another reason to celebrate the first Saturday in May: his wedding anniversary. He and his fiancee, Katie, decided to combine two important events — their wedding and their 2007 Derby party. They actually timed their ceremony and "I do's" around the Derby post time so that the wedding guests could make their Derby bets and watch the race on wireless broadband right there at the reception.

The entire reception had a Derby theme. The dinner tables were named for past Derby winners such as Secretariat, Spectacular Bid, and Smarty Jones. Centerpieces of big, shining silver pitchers held massive bouquets of red roses and fresh mint, and the dinner menu was — no surprise — distinctly Derby Day food, ending with minia-ture Derby pies as part of the dessert.

For the bride, the groom, and their guests, it was the best Derby party yet and certainly the most memorable.

The week before the Kentucky Derby in Penobscot, Maine, Har-old Shaw takes a worried look at the bed of mint outside his kitchen window. It's been a very cold winter, and he's afraid his backyard crop might not be ready for the juleps at his annual Kentucky Derby party.

When Shaw and his wife, Sue, moved from Kentucky to Maine thirty-four years ago, the dishes were barely unpacked and the cur-tains not yet hung in their new house before Shaw planted a backyard bed of mint. "I had to be sure I'd get my mint julep on Derby Day," he said. "I couldn't take any chances."

Like so many other Kentuckians, Shaw couldn't imagine a Derby Day without a celebration. So, next, he set about arranging an annual neighborhood party.

"It took some persuasion," he admitted. "The winters are long here, and people aren't very interested in a Kentucky Derby party while there's still snow on the ground."

But Shaw persisted, and before long, on the first Saturday in May, friends and neighbors eagerly forged through the snow and often-frigid temperatures to clutch frost-coated glasses in their already-cold hands and quaff down Shaw's icy mint juleps. He warmed guests up with his "good ole" Kentucky burgoo; ran the win, place, and show betting pots for them; and even treated them to his solo version of "My Old Kentucky Home."

There was one deep disappointment for Shaw, however. None of his Northern guests would eat his beloved Kentucky country ham.

"I tried serving it," he said wistfully, "but no one except me could get past the saltiness."

Whether your guests like Kentucky ham or not, you can share Bluegrass State traditions and create some of your own at Derby time.

Chapter Four

AN INVITATION THEY CAN'T REFUSE

The first thing you must do is decide when and what your Derby party will be. Will it be a Derby Eve dinner, a Derby morning brunch, or a Derby afternoon get-together?

By far the most popular choice is Derby afternoon with guests gathering to watch the Run for the Roses on television.

You can make your party as elaborate or informal as you like, but think about this: Being invited to a dress-down party is nothing unusual for most people. Such laid-back, "just come casual" entertaining is now social S.O.P. Backyard barbecues or picnic dinners are the thing. So, why don't you give your guests something different and elegant. Ask them to dress up. Fill your house with special decorations, have flowers in every room, bring out your best silver and china, and make just-for-the-occasion drinks. Guaranteed: Your guests will still be talking about your party come Derby time next year!

YOU'RE invited...

Make sure your guests understand they are expected to dress up. Otherwise, some embarrassed soul is bound to show up in blue jeans and sneakers. Your invitations should include "Derby attire, please" with specific details such as: "Cocktail dresses for women. Suits or jackets and neckties for men."

But, wait, what about hats? After all, the Derby is famous for them.

That's true. There are "hats" and then there are "Derby hats," and the two are very different. Hats are worn usually to keep your head

---

PARTY TIP

Invite your guests to arrive two hours before Derby post time.

---

warm or to hide unruly locks. Derby hats are worn to make a fashion statement. They are not utilitarian and are never worn to keep your head warm or to cover up a bad hair day. Once upon a time, ladies wore hats to the track to protect their complexions, but now they have just one purpose: to be oohed and aahed over just one day of the year.

Some well-heeled women gladly pay milliners up to the high hundreds of dollars to custom create fabulous, big-as-table-tops concoctions of feathers and flowers. Other women dream up their

---

PARTY TIP

If you want your guests to dress up, make it clear on your invitation. Be specific: "Women are to wear hats and cocktail dresses or suits. Men are to wear suits and neckties."

Don't worry about being arbitrary. They'll love being part of such a well-dressed group. Go even further and ask the men to make their mandatory neckties "horsey" ones.

---

own headgear, grab a glue gun, and go wild with roses and ribbons. Either way, wearing a hat is as much a Kentucky Derby tradition as downing a mint julep. That applies to men as well. Nothing will add a GQ flip to a seersucker suit like a Panama straw hat.

If you want your guests to don Derby hats, say so on your invitations and then plan a hat contest. Let guests vote (by secret ballot, of course) for the "prettiest," "most unusual," "most becoming," etc. Winners get prizes.

Now, about those invitations.

If you live in Kentucky, that's easy. You'll find a big selection of colorful Derby party invitations at most stationery stores. These are ready for you to have printed or filled out by hand with the particulars of your party. If you don't live in Kentucky, you can order great-looking Derby invitations online from a slew of sources that will also print them for you.

If you would rather create you own invitations, use a Derby theme: Make them in the shape of a horse, a jockey cap, or a mint julep glass. A plain white card with a big red rose drawn on it would do just fine.

Now, a word of advice: Please, please invite as many people as your budget and space will allow. Derby parties are great icebreakers, so the more guests, the merrier the party. One veteran Derby host says the secret of his annual party's success is that he invites "a lot of interesting people who entertain each other."

Chapter Five

CREATING A MEMORABLE SETTING

As your guests will be dressing up for your Derby party, your house, patio, porch, and particularly your buffet table are expected to do the same. So bring out those silver platters, pitchers, and bowls that you got for wedding gifts and that have been living their lives ever since wrapped in plastic in some dark corner of your kitchen cabinets. Shine them up, pile them with biscuits, mound them with beef tenderloin, or fill them with flowers. They will add gleam and glamour to your table.

If you don't have any handsome silver pieces, then here is one of the very best tips you will ever get on throwing a great Derby party, or any other kind. Quick ... grab your phone book and look up "Party Supplies — Renting" in the Yellow Pages. These businesses can be your best friend when it comes to entertaining. Need a silver chafing dish or silver candlesticks? Rent them. Not enough matching plates for your guests? Rent them. Short on nice linen napkins or an oversized tablecloth? Not to worry. A rental company will deliver, and later pick up, almost anything you need for your party, aside from the food, drink, and guests. You can rent a few forks or a few hundred, a few dishes or dozens. There's even a bonus! The staffers at these businesses are happy to share party decoration ideas and suggestions.

When it comes to your Derby party table, think "abundance." This is one time when less is not more. Your table should look lavish! Decorate your table beautifully and memorably.

The red rose is the official Kentucky Derby flower. Nothing looks as extravagant as masses of the long-stemmed beauties in a silver or crystal vase, so use as many as you can afford. They get expensive and scarce around Derby time. Shop around and order early.

Picture two dozen (even better, three dozen, if you can possibly spring for it) deep red roses in a silver champagne cooler as your centerpiece. (No champagne cooler? You know where to call.) Picture this lush arrangement in the middle of your table, which you have covered with a gleaming black silk cloth and adorned with streamers of 3-inch-wide silver ribbons radiating from the center-piece down to the floor.

- Or ... how about a shining silvery-gray tablecloth with swags of red roses looped around all sides of the table and a big, handsome silver pitcher filled with roses?

- Or ... a floor-length cloth of white silk with streamers of rose-red ribbons to match the roses of the centerpiece?

- Or ... a tablecloth made of big squares of different brightly colored silks like the ones the Derby jockeys wear?

Sound complicated or hard to find? Not so.

PARTY TIP

Ask the flower shop where you buy your Derby red roses to put the stems in those individually sealed vials. When your party is over, you can give each guest a rose to take home.

Take your table dimensions and head to a fabric store, the kind that sells dress fabrics, not upholstery materials. In most such shops you will find a big selection of inexpensive, polyester fabrics that look exactly like luxurious, high-priced real satin. There are wonderful colors — a gray that shines like silver, black that gleams like Black Beauty's coat, and snowy white to show off your red roses. Remember, you're looking for the most inexpensive satin-look you can find. You might not want to wear it yourself, but your table will look great in it. Ask the sales person how much you will need to drape your table with a floor-length skirt. You may have to take your materials to a seamstress to be made if you don't sew yourself. Don't worry about hemming your cloth. Pinking shears will do the trick.

If you want the "jockey silks" look, buy smaller pieces of fabric and stitch them together in big patchwork squares.

Your next stop is a big crafts store, such as Michael's. Here you will find lush fake roses and greenery and people who can turn them into garlands or wreaths for you. Maybe you have a hot glue gun and know how to do this yourself. The long garlands of roses will look smashing looped around the edge of your table. Stitch or staple them onto the tablecloth. Have some rose wreaths made. Hang a big one on your front door, your patio, over the bar, over the fireplace, and on the door of the bathroom your guests will be using. If you have a staircase, drape it

PARTY TIP

The Derby is a celebration of the horse. Load up on horsey items such as photos, posters, and prints. Borrow a saddle and bridle from a horseback-riding friend. Pick up some real horseshoes at a farrier supply store.

with rose garlands! This is the day to "deck the halls" with roses!

If you use clear glass vases to hold your roses, fill them about half way up with fresh cranberries before adding water and flowers. The roses will look even more dramatic with their stems in a bed of red.

Bring out anything "horsey" you have. Start haunting modest antique malls, flea markets, and garage sales for old brass or ceramic horses. You'll find many of them. Cluster them together, and surround them with rose garlands on a table.

Buy a cement jockey statue for your front entrance, and put a wreath of roses around his neck.

Cut out horseshoes from cardboard. Cover them with aluminum foil or spray them with silver paint and paste them on the walkway leading up to your front door. Better yet, buy real horseshoes if you have a farrier supply store in your town.

Cover your front door with a big, bright Kentucky Derby poster, ordered from the Kentucky Derby Museum Gift Shop.

Check with that fabulous party supply-rental place. Many of them rent large artificial topiaries ... trees, bushes, some even in the shape of horses. Put one on either side of your front door and stud the topiary's greenery with lots and lots of roses, real or fake.

If your party is going to spill onto the porch or patio, decorate that space with big baskets of giant showy paper roses and real greenery.

For a more informal party, one clever hostess went to a farm supply store, bought big feedbags (the kind horse oats come in), and sewed them together for her party tablecloth. She spray-painted feed buckets in bright colors and filled them with roses for her centerpieces.

Remember ... abundance is the key. You want your guests to see and think Kentucky Derby wherever they look.

Chapter Six

THE JOYS OF MINT JULEPS

There is one sacred, unbreakable rule about any Kentucky Derby party: Mint juleps *must* be served. They are essential. Not to serve them would be as unthinkable as a Derby horse without a jockey. Or, as one clever fellow put it, "like a birthday party without a birthday cake." Unthinkable!

The mint julep is almost exclusively a Derby Day drink. You could hang out all year in cocktail lounges from Boston, Massachusetts, to Butte, Montana, and probably never hear a single person order "a mint julep, please." The famous drink's fame flares only one day a year — the first Saturday in May. The other 364 days, it's ignored, shunned like fruitcake after Christmas. But on Derby Day, *everybody* drinks mint juleps. Even people who don't like them and who complain they taste like "green mouthwash" drink them. Since 1938, mint juleps have been the official drink of the Kentucky Derby, and Churchill Downs sells more than 120,000 of them over Derby weekend.

How and when and where the mint julep was born is a popular, old, and friendly argument. Entire books have been written about the drink's origin. It is believed to have first been served way back in the early 1700s. Maryland, Georgia, Virginia, and Kentucky all have fiercely claimed its beginnings, but today the general public has come to consider it a true Kentucky tradition, evoking those old Hollywood movie images of parties on the plantation lawn, hoop-skirted ladies, and white-coated servants passing around long, cool drinks on silver trays.

As for the mint itself, a popular Kentucky legend credits a long-ago Mississippi River boatman who went ashore to find some clean, fresh spring water to add to his bourbon. When he spotted a patch of mint growing by the water, he added a sprig to his drink and, voilà, the mint julep was born! What a happy day!

The debate over how to make, and how to serve, a proper mint julep never ends. How much ice, sugar, mint, and bourbon to use is a well-worn and well-loved Kentucky controversy. While julep makers and drinkers have their own favorite recipes, there are a couple of absolutely rigid rules concerning things *not* allowed. After all, you don't tinker with perfection.

PARTY TIP

Make sure that whoever is tending bar actually
knows how to make a mint julep.
Have a practice run before your guests arrive.

Number one: You must not use any liquor except bourbon. No scotch, no gin, no rum, no vodka. Bourbon *only* and preferably *Kentucky* bourbon. The state is famous for it.

Number two: No green stuff except *mint* is allowed in the drink. This means no substitutes. I say this because so many trendy recipes call for "adventurous use of greens" as drink garnishes. But this is not the time to get adventurous. You're mixing a mint julep, not a salad. So no getting jazzy with the cilantro or parsley just because it's green and you couldn't find fresh mint in your supermarket.

As for the rest, it's up to you. Your julep-making can be as complicated or simple as you like. You can cook up your own mint-sugar

---

PARTY TIP

Buy Derby swizzle sticks for the juleps. Order them online from the Kentucky Derby Museum Gift Shop.

syrup or buy it ready-made in a bottle at a liquor/party store. No one will ever know and besides that, it's good. If you have a large crowd coming to your party, you can even mix pitchers full of the finished juleps, bourbon added and all, so they're ready to pour into glasses, which you've packed half full with shaved ice. This do-ahead method could lead to leftovers, but is that really a problem?

Mint juleps are usually served in special glasses or "julep cups." Once upon a time, those cups were made of sterling silver, but rising silver prices have made them so valuable that some hosts understandably hesitate to use them. Instead, they buy souvenir Kentucky Derby glasses (not plastic, but real glass, imagine that!) at a party store or order them from the Kentucky Derby Museum Gift Shop at Churchill Downs. Guests can take these home with them as attractive, useful memorabilia of your party and, what's more, the glasses will actually increase in value each year. Prices can range from a few dollars for recent editions to several hundred for rare glasses, according to *Kentucky Derby Glasses Price Guide*.

If you prefer plastic glasses for a large party (and many hosts do), you'll find good-looking mock silver julep cups at a party store. But, please, don't even *think* about serving Kentucky's most revered drink in a paper cup or, horrors, a styrofoam one! Famous Kentuckians such as statesman Henry Clay and writer Irvin S. Cobb would spin like tops in their graves. Both of them spent years perfecting their julep recipes.

Found in one of his diaries, Clay's was almost exquisitely poetic. Here it is, and it's believed to be the same one he used when he served the first mint julep in Washington, D.C., to friends in the bar of the Willard Hotel back in the early 1800s. In honor of the great statesman, the hotel still uses his recipe for this signature drink, which is available all year-round.

The mint leaves, fresh and tender, should be pressed against a coin-silver goblet with the back of a silver spoon. Only bruise the leaves gently and then remove them from the goblet. Half fill with cracked ice. Mellow bourbon, aged in oaken barrels, is poured from the jigger and allowed to slide slowly through the cracked ice.

In another receptacle, granulated sugar is slowly mixed into chilled limestone water to make a silvery mixture as smooth as some rare Egyptian oil, then poured on top of the ice. While beads of moisture gather on the burnished exterior of the silver goblet, garnish the brim of the goblet with the choicest sprigs of mint.

Wow! Statesman Clay's recipe might have enticed temperance leader Carrie Nation herself to have "well, maybe just one."

Bill Samuels' mint julep recipe isn't quite as flowery as Henry Clay's, but it's equally as appealing and a heck of a lot easier. Samuels is the president/CEO of Maker's Mark, the world-famous Kentucky bourbon. His father started the company, and Bill grew up singing the praises of Kentucky in general and Maker's Mark in particular. His julep recipe is "hands on."

Bill Samuels' Special Mint Julep

1 bottle Maker's Mark (90-proof bourbon whisky)

fresh mint

water, preferably distilled

granulated sugar

garnish with mint sprigs and powdered sugar (optional)

1. MINT EXTRACT

To prepare the mint extract, pick the mint and remove leaves smaller than a dime. Wash; pat dry. Put 40 leaves in a mixing bowl and cover with 3 ounces of Maker's Mark.

Allow leaves to soak in bourbon for 15 minutes.

Gather leaves in a bundle; put in a clean cotton cloth and wring vigorously over the mixing bowl, bruising leaves. Continue dipping the cloth in bourbon (several times) and wringing the leaves so the mint juice drips back into the bourbon. Let this mint extract sit.

2. SIMPLE SYRUP

Mix equal amounts of granulated sugar and water in a cooking pot. (Example: 1 cup sugar and 1 cup water) Heat long enough for the sugar to dissolve in the water. Stir so the sugar doesn't burn. Remove from heat and let cool. This can be done several hours in advance.

3. JULEP MIXTURE

Pour 3½ parts Maker's Mark to 1 part simple syrup into a large bowl. Begin adding mint extract in small portions. You must taste and smell — there is no formula as each extract will vary in strength. (Author's note: Take your time here. No rushing the tasting. This is fun!)

Pour finished julep stock into a covered jar and refrigerate at least 24 hours to "marry" the flavors.

4. SERVING THE JULEP

To serve the julep, fill each silver julep cup half full with shaved ice. Insert a mint sprig.

Pack in more ice to about 1 inch over the top of the cup. Insert a straw that has been cut to no more than 1 inch above the top of cup so guests must sniff the "bloom" as they are sipping their juleps.

When frost forms on the cup or glass, pour refrigerated julep mixture over the ice and sprinkle powdered sugar on top if desired.

You have made a perfect mint julep the Bill Samuels way.

If Bill's recipe is too complicated for you, try this easy one that is a favorite of many bartenders.

Mint Julep

Makes 1 drink. Multiply as needed to make required quantity for your party.

3 to 4 ounces bourbon (Yes, that much for 1 drink. This julep is not for the faint hearted.)

1 ounce mint-flavored simple syrup, available in bottles or make your own (See Bill Samuels' recipe.)

lots of shaved ice (available in bags at party, convenience, or grocery stores)

- -

mint leaves and mint sprigs for garnish

- -

DIRECTIONS

Pour ½ ounce of the mint-flavored simple syrup into a glass or julep cup. If the mint taste is not strong enough for you, stir some of the mint leaves into it. Pack the glass or cup full with shaved ice. Pour the remaining ½ ounce of syrup over the ice. Then, pour on the 3 to 4 ounces of bourbon. Garnish with a mint sprig. Sip through a straw.

Count on it. There are bound to be some nondrinkers among your party guests. More and more people these days choose not to imbibe,

> **PARTY TIP**
>
> Remember, you need shaved or crushed ice,
>
> not ice cubes, for mint juleps.

but you are the host who thinks of everything and you will make sure they won't have to miss out on the drink of Derby Day. You can serve them this terrific, no-alcohol mint julep. In their take-home souvenir glass, of course.

Virgin Mint Julep

Makes 1 drink. Multiply as needed to make required quantity

¼ cup water

¼ cup granulated sugar

1 tablespoon chopped fresh mint leaves

2 cups crushed or shaved ice

½ cup prepared lemonade

fresh mint sprigs

In a small saucepan, combine water, sugar, and chopped mint leaves. Cook over low heat until the sugar dissolves. Remove from heat and let cool (about 1 hour).

When cool, strain mint leaves out.

Fill frozen glasses or julep cups (which have been placed in freezer) with crushed or shaved ice. Pour the lemonade into each glass and add a healthy splash of sugar-mint syrup. Garnish with a mint sprig.

Mint juleps won't be the only drink you serve, you understand. They truly are an acquired taste, and there will be guests who would rather drink a glass of mint-flavored cough syrup. Nevertheless, most of the crowd will want not just one but "another" julep, or more, so plan accordingly. This is the day that mint juleps live for, their once-a-year day to shine. So drink up, and when the strains of "My Old Kentucky Home" begin to play, raise a julep toast to the hallowed, high-proof tradition of the Kentucky Derby and the state that fathered it.

Chapter Seven

KENTUCKY CLASSICS — DON'T COUNT CALORIES

Think "party," and the next word that pops into your mind is "food." If you are the host, your prime question is "what will I serve?"

Here's a tip: This is a Kentucky Derby party you are planning, so even if you are famous for your Mexican fiesta salsa dip, or if your friends go absolutely gaga over your Lebanese stuffed grape leaves, please do not serve them. Save them for another party. Forgo them in favor of traditional Kentucky dishes. There are so many wonderful, seasonal foods associated with Kentucky in the springtime. Concentrate on them, and your guests will gobble them up with delight.

Another tip: Kentucky Derby treats are rich in calories. Leave them that way. A Derby party is not the time to switch low-fat cheese or skim milk for the real thing in recipes or to fret over fat

grams. Take the motto of
that most famous of
southern belles,
Scarlett O'Hara:
"I'll think about
that tomorrow."
After all, the Derby
and its food come only
one day a year. So enjoy it.

What you serve will naturally depend upon what kind of party you give. For a Derby Eve dinner, think Kentucky burgoo or fried chicken and corn pudding. For a Derby breakfast, a traditional creamed-egg and mushroom casserole with cheese grits would be perfect. However, those dishes require using knives and forks and balancing plates of hot food. So, let's focus instead on foods for the most popular kind of Derby party, the type you are most likely to host — an afternoon event where "finger foods" are the thing to serve. Mind you, these are not dainty little "bites" of this and that. Not at all. No "tea party" stuff allowed. Your menu will be substantial with beef, ham, shrimp, and chicken. Your guests will be contentedly full and, best of all, you will not have spent your precious party time running back and forth to the kitchen trying to keep things hot.

Here are some recipes from the famous Kentucky cookbook, *Entertaining with Bluegrass Winners,* from the Garden Club of Lexington, as well as a few from extraordinarily good cooks who haven't, but could, publish their own cookbooks. By the way, all these recipes are for dishes that would be as perfect at Derby dinners and brunches as they are for afternoon parties.

One of the dishes that you'll see on almost every Derby party table is beef tenderloin. This old standby is easy to prepare, easy to serve, and always what the buffet guests seem to head for first. Here is Keeneland Race Course's Rosemary Garlic Beef Tenderloin with Horseradish Sauce.

Rosemary Garlic Beef Tenderloin

Serves 10 to 12

1 beef tenderloin, trimmed and cleaned

MARINADE

3 tablespoons chopped garlic

1 tablespoon cracked black pepper

1 cup vegetable oil

½ cup balsamic vinegar

2 tablespoons kosher salt

¼ cup fresh chopped rosemary

Combine marinade ingredients in a bowl.

Rub this mixture on the tenderloin and marinate in refrigerator for at least 6 hours.

Before cooking meat, remove from refrigerator and allow tenderloin to stand at room temperature for 30 minutes.

Preheat oven to 500°F. Place tenderloin in a roasting pan and insert a meat thermometer. Reduce oven temperature to 350°F when you put tenderloin in. Bake for 20 minutes or until the meat thermometer registers 120°F. The meat will be rare but will continue to cook a little after you remove it from the oven.

Let the tenderloin sit for about 15 to 20 minutes before slicing.

Serve with horseradish sauce.

HORSERADISH SAUCE

½ cup mayonnaise

½ cup heavy cream, whipped

⅛ teaspoon dry mustard

⅓ cup prepared horseradish, drained

Tabasco sauce to taste

Worcestershire sauce to taste

Combine mayonnaise and whipped cream.

Stir in dry mustard and horseradish.

Season lightly with Tabasco and Worcestershire sauce to taste. Serve with tenderloin.

Lou Ann Moss of Lexington, Kentucky, says her tenderloin recipe gives the old standby a special punch.

Marinated Beef Tenderloin

Serves 8 to 10

(7 to 8 lbs.) beef tenderloin, trimmed and cleaned

MARINADE

1 envelope Good Seasons Dry Italian Salad Dressing Mix

½ cup water

½ cup ketchup

1 teaspoon dry mustard

¼ teaspoon Worchestershire sauce

Coat tenderloin in marinade, turning often. Marinate overnight in the refrigerator. Allow meat to reach room temperature before cooking in preheated 425°F oven for 30 minutes or until internal temperature reaches 140°F on meat thermometer.

Serve with Henry Bain Sauce.

If you're not from Kentucky, you may never have heard of Henry Bain Sauce, the classic condiment that is named for its creator. For decades Henry Bain was the distinguished headwaiter at the private, prestigious Pendennis Club in Louisville. He conjured up this very spicy sauce specifically for beef way back in 1881.

The recipe is a deep secret. Mr. Bain's family reportedly keeps it that way. You can now buy Henry Bain sauce, or at least, something close to it, bottled, in gourmet stores. If you want to make it yourself, here's the recipe from *Entertaining with Bluegrass Winners* cookbook.

HENRY BAIN SAUCE

1 (14 -ounce) bottle ketchup

1 (12-ounce) bottle chili sauce

1 (10-ounce) bottle A-1 Steak Sauce

1 (10-ounce) bottle Worcestershire sauce

1 (8-ounce) bottle Major Grey's Chutney

2 tablespoons Tabasco sauce

Combine all ingredients, mixing well, and pour into bottles. The sauce can be refrigerated for months.

Or, how about sending your party guests home with a small bottle as a party souvenir?

Mention Kentucky Derby cooking and immediately, country ham on beaten biscuits springs to many people's minds. That is, unless they have actually eaten a beaten biscuit, or tried to eat one. At the risk of being asked to turn in my Kentucky Colonel card, let me say that the best thing about a beaten biscuit is watching folks bite into one for the first time. It's fascinating to see their looks of eager anticipation turn first to bewilderment, then to deep distaste, and finally to panic as they look frantically around for a place to discard the lump of chalk.

There are still purists in Kentucky who sit happily at their antique beaten biscuit presses and roll out dozens and dozens of the rock-like pellets, convinced that people just can't get enough of them. But take my word, your guests will be happier and your country ham will taste better on soft biscuits. There's no need to spend hours making these yourself, no matter how proud you are of your biscuit-making skills. You're going to need a lot of these, so turn to your best local bakery or a to restaurant such as Cracker Barrel, which will sell you its delicious famous country biscuits by the dozen. Bob Evans, KFC, and Hardee's also sell their biscuits by the dozen. Order a day or two ahead to make sure they'll have them ready. Split them, butter them lightly, and pile them on a silver tray. Perfect! And you didn't even have to turn on your oven.

If you insist, you can cook the country ham yourself, but again, other people can do it for you beautifully. Gourmet food shops, caterers, even supermarket deli departments will cook and slice your ham in just the right-sized, paper-thin pieces to fit on a biscuit. If you don't live in a southern state, you might have to special order your country ham from your butcher or even online.

Keep in mind that "aged hams," as they're also called, have a distinctly pungent taste and are very, very, very salty. It is a delicious treat, but most Northerners prefer non-aged "city" hams. (Every southerner has heard the story of the New York City woman who was shipped a gift of a country ham from friends in the South and threw it in the garbage because she thought it was "spoiled" with "all that mold" on it.)

If you want to take the time, here's a traditional recipe for baked Kentucky country ham.

Baked Kentucky Country Ham

An 8-pound ham, thinly sliced after cooking, will be enough to make 100 ham-and-biscuit sandwiches.

1 country ham, preferably about 18 months old

¼ cup whole cloves (reserve some for decoration)

1 cup brown sugar

1 cup vinegar

1½ gallons water

Scrub ham with a stiff brush to remove any mold. Immerse, skin side up, in cold water and soak overnight. Sprinkle cloves in the bottom of a large roaster. Add ham, fat side up, and stick reserved cloves in the fat. Add brown sugar, vinegar, and water to the roaster.

Cover and bake at 375°F for 1 hour. Lower heat to 275°F, and bake an additional 20 minutes per pound. Cool. Trim off fat. If desired, remove the bone and tie ham securely with string. Refrigerate overnight. Remove string; cover ham with topping and bake at 350°F until the topping is browned.

TOPPING

1 cup brown sugar, packed

1 cup cornmeal

1 tablespoon ground cloves

1 teaspoon ground cinnamon

Combine ingredients and mix thoroughly.

For years, spicy barbecued shrimp has been a favorite at Churchill Downs during Derby time, and it would be a sure winner with your guests. This recipe should serve 16, but you know how people gobble up any shrimp dish, so double, triple, or quadruple as needed.

Oven-Barbecued Shrimp

Serves 16

1 pound butter

1 pound margarine

1 teaspoon dried rosemary

¾ cup Worcestershire sauce

5 tablespoons black pepper

4 teaspoons salt

4 lemons, thinly sliced

1 teaspoon Tabasco sauce

10 pounds raw, unpeeled, headless, medium-to-large shrimp

Combine all ingredients except shrimp and heat to boiling. Place shrimp in shallow pan and pour the sauce over them. Bake, uncovered, at 400°F for 20 minutes, stirring twice during cooking. Serve with the sauce.

Fried Chicken — The Easy Way

Almost everyone adores fried chicken, and this is the right day to serve *real* fried chicken. Not *oven* fried, but floured and fried the old-fashioned southern way — in fat until the skin is as crisp as a potato chip. This is the fried chicken people dream about, and you can serve platters of it without getting a single splatter of fat on you or your stove.

KFC or any other take-out chicken restaurant sells perfectly delicious fried chicken wings, bone-in or bone-out, that are just the right size for your finger food buffet. Your guests will devour these, so order dozens of them. Pick them up an hour before the party and re-crisp them in a 250°F oven.

You could add two lovely "extras" to your buffet. May is asparagus time as well as Derby time in Kentucky.

Asparagus Roll-Ups

Serves 12

12 slices white bread, with crusts on

2 tablespoons chopped chives

1 (8-ounce) carton whipped cream cheese

8 slices bacon, cooked, drained, and crumbled

¼ cup melted butter
24 spears asparagus

Flatten bread with rolling pin. Mix cream cheese, chives, and crumbled bacon. Spread on bread slices. Place two spears of asparagus on each slice of bread and roll up. Cut into four bite-sized pieces or leave whole, if you wish. Place seam-side down on buttered cookie sheet, brush with melted butter, and bake at 400°F for 12 minutes or until crisp. These don't have to be served right away. They can be kept warm in a chafing dish and are still delicious even when served at room temperature.

"Green cheese" doesn't sound very appetizing, but ever since a Louisville caterer dreamed up this Benedictine spread back in the 1920s, these little sandwiches have been a Derby food classic. Kentuckians can buy the spread at gourmet or grocery stores. If you live elsewhere, you may have to make it from scratch, but it's worth it. Just don't overdo the green food coloring. You're not cooking for a St. Patrick's Day party.

Benedictine Sandwiches

Makes enough spread for 8 sandwiches.
Cut into quarters, they will serve 8 to 10 people.

1 medium-sized cucumber, peeled and seeded

1 (8-ounce) package cream cheese, softened

½ medium onion, finely chopped or ground

dash salt

dash red pepper or Tabasco sauce

green food coloring

white bread, thinly sliced

Grind cucumber in a blender. Place on cheesecloth and squeeze out the juice. Combine pulp with cream cheese, onion, salt, and red pepper or Tabasco sauce. Mix thoroughly. Add a very small amount of food coloring — just enough to make the spread a very pale green. Spread on thin slices of white sandwich bread. Cut into quarters.

Add a big, beautiful tray of cheeses and crackers to your buffet table and you're done. Except for the one thing that hardly anyone passes up at a party — dessert.

Kentuckians will tell you the tastiest way to top off a Derby dinner is with a slice of Derby Pie, a luscious chocolate-nut concoction dreamed up in 1954 by the Kern family of Louisville for their Melrose Inn Restaurant. The pie was such a success and was copied so much that Kern's Kitchen trademarked the name in 1968. No one else dares use it without risking a lawsuit. The family once sued *Bon Appetit* magazine for running a Derby Pie recipe in a cookbook and won. The secret recipe is still known only to the family and one trusted employee. The Kerns sell about 130,000 pies each year, most at Derby time. There are slews of similar recipes with different names, but for the sake of tradition, it would be fun to order the "real thing." Order online, and Kerns will send your pie frozen. Cut it into small squares instead of slices so your buffet guests won't need forks.

Entertaining with Bluegrass Winners cookbook has this recipe.

Chocolate Pecan Pie with a Shot

Serves 6 to 8

1 flaky pie crust

pecan pie filling

PECAN PIE FILLING

3 tablespoons all-purpose flour

½ cup unsalted butter, melted

½ cup sugar

½ cup dark corn syrup

2 large eggs, beaten

2 tablespoons Kentucky bourbon

¼ teaspoon salt

2 cups pecans, chopped & toasted

1 cup chopped semi-sweet chocolate

1 egg with 1 teaspoon water

whipped cream, for garnish

Preheat oven to 350°F.

On a lightly floured surface, roll out pie crust, fit into a 9-inch pie pan, crimp the edges, and place in freezer for 15 minutes.

Line pie crust with parchment paper, and fill with pie weights or dry beans. Bake for 20 minutes; then remove the paper and pie weights, and allow crust to cool.

By hand, stir flour, butter, sugar, corn syrup, eggs, bourbon, and salt in medium bowl. Stir in pecans and chocolate. Pour into crust.

Whisk egg and water and brush over the edges of the pie.

Bake for 40 minutes. Allow to cool. Serve with a dollop of whipped cream.

Chapter Eight

POST TIME

t's the first Saturday in May, and you are in the starting gate of your Kentucky Derby party, ready and eager to go.

Plan to kick off your party two hours before the Derby post time. Have your bar open, the julep glasses chilled, and your television sets turned on and tuned into network Derby coverage when your first guests arrive.

Make *sure* you have enough TV sets. Rent more if you don't. One for each room is best, and for heaven's sake, check them the day before to make sure both video and audio are working right. Your

> ### PARTY TIP
> Have television sets in every area or room where your guests will be. If you don't have enough TVs, rent some. Have them turned on and tuned in to network pre-Derby coverage when guests arrive.

guests won't wait until race time to watch TV. All afternoon they'll want to catch snatches of interviews with horse owners, trainers, and racing pundits. The crowds that pack Churchill Downs put on a great show. On Derby Day, the sky's the limit when it comes to fancy clothes, bizarre hats, and the uninhibited antics of the infield fans. So keep all of your TV sets on during the party.

Just as a mint julep needs bourbon, a Derby party needs *betting* to give it a real "kick." You can make your party betting as simple

PARTY TIP

If you plan to hold your party outside on the lawn, terrace, patio, or porch, have a back-up emergency plan so that everything can be moved inside quickly and without confusion if it rains.

or as complicated as you like. Guests will love it either way, whether they pick their horse on blind luck or through handicapping skills.

The simplest way is the winner-take-all "pot" system. Each Derby horse's name is written on a slip of paper. All the slips are then mixed up and put into an envelope or a hat. (You might use pretty flowered and feathered "Derby" hats for this.) For $2, say, a guest gets to draw a name. After the race the lucky person who drew the winning horse collects the entire pot. As the Derby field is limited to no more than

---

PARTY TIP

Pass out copies of the lyrics to "My Old Kentucky Home" and have everyone stand and sing along with the Churchill Downs crowd. Follow the charming tradition of one Kentucky family that has had three generations of Derby Day get-togethers. Just before the singing of "My Old Kentucky Home," everyone stands and raises mint juleps in a communal toast "to the future." Lovely!

> **PARTY TIP**
>
> Take pictures. Lots of them! If you're asking people to
>
> dress up, show them how good they look.
>
> Make sure the guests receive their photos.

20 horses, obviously you will need more than one pot to give all your guests a chance to bet. Ten or more pots are not unusual, and people can buy into as many as they wish. You might offer $2, $3, and $5 pots. Ask early arrivals at your party to act as cashiers, selling the bets and then paying off the winners. This is really a fun way to bet, with guests who drew longshots cheering for their horses.

If you want to make things slightly more complicated, you could also have "place" and "show" pots. Same deal — the winning slip takes the entire pot.

You could also set up an actual mini-pari-mutuel pool. Sell "win" tickets only, charge $2, and let guests buy as many tickets as they wish. This method gives them the chance to "pick" their horse. After the race, winners turn in their tickets, the tickets are counted, and the total amount of money wagered on the Derby winner is divided equally.

Some hosts go for more elaborate betting. Arlene and Harry Cohen of Lexington, Kentucky, had a big plywood replica of Churchill Downs' famous Twin Spires built to use as the betting cage at their annual Derby party. There are two betting windows with cashiers on full-time duty and even a "real, live bookmaker," Arlene said, to take the bets and set up the odds. "Well, he wasn't actually a bookmaker. More like an actuary," she laughed. "We made sure he was legal."

PARTY TIP

Have as many door prizes as you can afford. People love to get presents. Cover a shoebox with silver paper, glue on big red paper roses, and have every guest draw a number. Announce the winners and pass out the prizes after the Derby and the buffet.

Pop around to your local newsstand and pick up some Derby Day copies of the *Daily Racing Form*. Even if your guests are simply drawing a horse from a pot, they'll still enjoy seeing what the different handicappers have to say about their picks' chances to win.

Be sure to clip out any newspaper articles on the Derby horses and have these handy on a table for your guests to read. The sports pages are loaded with these "color pieces" during Derby week.

Hire a fortune teller. Even if she (or he) may not be able to foresee which horse will win the Derby, your guests will love having their futures predicted.

Post time for the Kentucky Derby traditionally is just after 6 p.m. Eastern Standard Time. If you live on the West Coast, this means the race will be run near 3 p.m. Regardless, the best time to open your buffet is about 15 minutes after the race is over. This will give your guests time to watch the replay, the interview with the winning jockey, and the governor's presentation of the trophy and the blanket of roses. Then it's "They're Off" time again — this time to the table!

Door Prizes

- A bottle of good Kentucky bourbon
- DVDs of the movies *Seabiscuit* and *Dreamer*
- A box of bourbon ball candy, made in Kentucky
  Order online.
- A mint plant in a pretty little ceramic pot
- A cookbook featuring Kentucky recipes such as *Entertaining with Bluegrass Winners*. Order online from Amazon.com, from Exclusively-Equine.com, or from your bookstore.

Shop online at the Derby Museum Gift Shop for such things as:

- Equestrian calendars with great photos of Derby winners or beautiful Kentucky horse farms
- Derby bracelets, cuff links, or tietacks
- Derby salt and pepper shakers

Chapter Nine

DERBY BITS & PIECES

MINT JULEP TRIVIA

In preparation for the Derby weekend,
Churchill Downs buys close to 900 dozen
bunches of fresh mint, estimated to be enough to provide
a sprig for 150,000 juleps.

Churchill Downs' gardeners are said to have
planted mint outside the track clubhouse back in
1875 so that mint juleps
could be served at the first Kentucky Derby.

The owner of the Kentucky Derby winner receives a specially
designed sterling-silver julep cup.

The directors room at Churchill Downs contains
a complete set of silver julep cups,
each one engraved with the name of the winner,
starting with Aristides in 1875.

In 1905 only three horses ran in the Kentucky Derby, the smallest field in the race's history. Agile was the winner.

Derby horses are all 3-year-olds. No horse has won the Derby without racing at the age of 2 since Apollo in 1882.

The Kentucky Derby is the second-oldest organized sporting event in the nation. Only the Travers Stakes at Saratoga is older.

The winning jockey of the first Kentucky Derby was African-American rider Oliver Lewis on a colt named Aristides.

Between 1875 and 1902, African-American jockeys won 15 of the 28 Derbies.

The youngest jockeys ever to win the Derby were 15-year-olds Alonzo "Lonnie" Clayton in 1892 and James "Soup" Perkins in 1895.

The only horse to win the Derby and later be
disqualified was Dancer's Image in 1968, after tests
showed traces of a banned anti-inflammatory drug
in his urine.

The fastest Derby time was set in 1973 by the famed
Triple Crown winner Secretariat. His record time was
1:59 ⅖ seconds for the 1¼ miles.

The first gray horse to win the Derby was Determine, in 1954.

The Kentucky Derby has been postponed only once.
That was in 1945 during World War II. That year it was run in
June instead of the traditional May.

In 1952 the Kentucky Derby was covered on national
television for the first time.

The governor of Kentucky is the only person permitted to present the Kentucky Derby trophy to the winner.

The first woman to ride in the Derby was Diane Crump, in 1970.

The oldest jockey to win the Derby was Bill Shoemaker. He was 54 when he rode Ferdinand to victory in 1986.

Some of the most famous horses in history never ran in the Kentucky Derby, including Man o' War, Seabiscuit, and John Henry.

MUSIC TRIVIA

"My Old Kentucky Home" has been played before the race for more than seventy years, usually by the University of Louisville's marching band.

Pop singer Dan Fogelberg wrote and recorded "Run for the Roses" for the 1980 Derby.

A FINAL WORD

So, now your party's post time is here! Everything is ready. The julep glasses are frosting, the delicious scents of roses and fresh mint fill the air, and your first guests are knocking on your Derby-decorated front door. Your party is "off and running."

Now it's time for you to relax, mingle with your happy guests, and have as much fun as they will, but when they aren't looking, you just might want to raise your mint julep in a quiet little toast of congratulation to yourself. You deserve it because you really know how to throw a great Derby party!

ABOUT THE AUTHOR

Sue Wylie is one of Kentucky's best-known and respected broadcast journalists. She is in the Kentucky Broadcasting Hall of Fame and has received the coveted "Kentucky Mike Award" from the Kentucky Associated Press for broadcast excellence.

For the past decade Wylie has entertained and informed radio listeners with her top-rated *Sue Wylie Show*, heard throughout Kentucky each weekday morning on WVLK-AM in Lexington.

A local celebrity who is prominent on the social scene, Wylie has been a regular guest at Kentucky's famous Derby parties over the years. Her rare access to Bluegrass hostesses has made her a Derby party authority.

Wylie has spent her entire career in broadcasting, which she studied at the Cincinnati College/Conservatory of Music. She began her career with the network affiliates in Cincinnati and later became one of the first women in Florida to do "hard news," reporting at the NBC station in Miami.

In Lexington, Kentucky, she hosted the NBC-TV affiliate's popular *Noon Today* for more than 25 years. She is best known for hosting and producing the weekly Kentucky political program *Your Government*.

In addition to her daily radio show, Wylie is a freelance writer and a sought-after political commentator.